WISDOM for little brains

What is a proverb?

Proverbs are wise sayings.
They are usually popular, memorable, short
and to the point and give good advice.
Proverbs also contain simple truths that
help us learn from others' experiences.

How to use?

A little pocket book for those who enjoy reading and coloring.

What's more? They are a wonderful source of wisdom and knowledge on a whole slew of topics. Packed full of valuable proverbs and tips to help you in life. There's a saying: "A picture is worth a thousand words" and so maybe one of these pictures will stick in your head as you read, think about and color it. Then, try to putting it into ACTION, today!

Learn to control yourself. A man without self-control is like a building without walls.

(25:28)

My child, listen to your father's teaching.
And do not forget your mother's advice. (1:8)

Be grateful for your possessions and you will have what you need. (3:9-10)

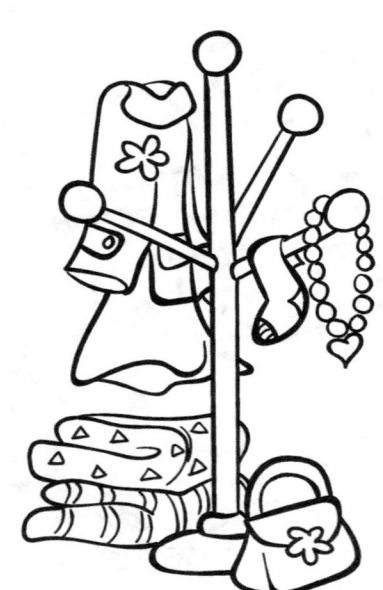

Those who work hard will have abundant food, but those who do only what they want miss out.

(12:11)

Important people are pleased with those who speak honest words. You will be valued and respected if you speak the truth. (16:13)

A lazy person will end up poor. But a hard worker will become rich.

(10:4)

A righteous person takes good care of his his animals. He is gentle and kind.

(12:10)

Those who listen to good advice will live in safety. They will be safe, without fear of being hurt.

(1:33)

Wise people are rewarded with wealth. (14:24)

People who are proud will be ruined. But those who are humble will be honored.

(18:12)

Too much talking may cause you to say the wrong things. Wise people know when it's time to keep quiet.

(10:19)

A wise person can look forward to good times. But an evil person can expect nothing.

(10:28)

Worry makes a person feel as if he is carrying a heavy load. But a kind word cheers them up.

(12:25)

In all work
there is
reward.

(14:23)

The way of the good person is like the light of dawn. It grows brighter and brighter until it is fully day.

(4:18)

A friend loves you all the time. they will be there when you need help.

(17:17)

The mind of a smart person is ready to get knowledge. The wise person listens to learn more.

(18:15)

Patience is better than strength. Controlling your temper is better than capturing a city.

(16:32)

Don't ever stop being kind and truthful. Let kindness and truth show in all you do.

(3:3)

Getting good advice from others helps you to succeed in life.

(15:22)

A person
who accepts
correction
will be
honored.

(13:18)

It's better to have a small simple meal where there is love than a fancy feast without love.

(15:17)

Whenever you are able, do good to people who need help.

(3:27)

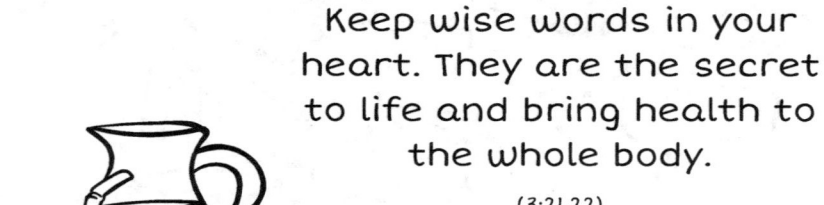

Keep wise words in your heart. They are the secret to life and bring health to the whole body.

(3:21,22)

Wisdom will make your life more pleasant for you and others.

(3:17)

Good sense will protect you. Understanding will guard you and keep you safe.

(2:11,12)

Do your best to remember all that you have learned. It is the most important thing in your life.

(4:13)

A gentle answer will calm a person's anger. But an unkind answer will cause more anger.

(15:1)

Happy is he who finds wisdom,
and who seeks to understand.
For Wisdom is even more
precious than silver or gold.

(3:13-15)

Keep your
eyes focused
on the right
thing to do.

(4:25)

By listening you will understand what is honest and fair. You will know what is the right thing to do.

(2:9)

My child, don't forget wise teaching. Keep it in mind. Then you will live a long time and your life will be successful.

(3:1-2)

Pleasant words are
like a honeycomb.
They make a person
happy and healthy.

(16:24)

A person who gives to others will get richer. Whoever helps others will himself be helped.

(11:25)

Hatred stirs up trouble. But love forgives all wrongs.

(10:12)

Whoever forgives someone's mistakes makes a friend.

(17:9)

A wise person shows others how to be wise too.

(11:30)

A wise and obedient child makes his parents glad.

(10:1b)

A wise person pays attention to the instructions of others. This will help him live a happy life.

(15:31)

A person will
be rewarded
for not only
what he says
but also for
what he does.

(12:14)

Wisdom is pleasing. If you find it, you have hope for the future and your wishes will come true.

(24:14)

Saying the right word at the right time is pleasant. Smart people think before they answer.

(15:23,28)

Be very careful about what you think. Your thoughts run your life.

(4:23)

Listen to wisdom. Try with all your heart to gain understanding.

(2:2)

As a tree gives us fruit, healing words, kind and gentle words give us life.

(15:4)

A happy heart is like good medicine. But a hurtful spirit drains your strength.

(17:22)

Happiness makes a person smile. But sadness makes a person's spirit feel down.

(2:13)

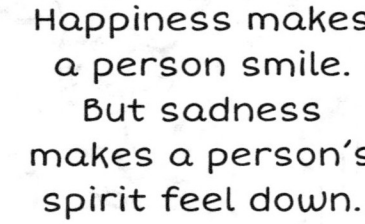

In wisdom is safety. You won't need to be afraid when you lie down. Your sleep will be sweet.

(3:24)

Visit our website www.iCharacter.org
for more great books and
even some free videos.

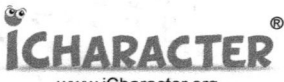

Published by iCharacter Limited ®. (Ireland)
By Agnes and Salem de Bezenac
Illustrated by Agnes de Bezenac
Copyright 2019. All rights reserved.
All Bible verses adapted from the KJV.
www.iCharacter.org

Copyright © 2019 by iCharacter Limited ®. All rights reserved. No part of this book may be reproduced in any form or by any electronic or mechanical means, including information storage and retrieval systems, without written permission from the publisher or author, except in the case of a reviewer, who may quote brief passages embodied in critical articles or in a review.

www.ingramcontent.com/pod-product-compliance
Lightning Source LLC
Chambersburg PA
CBHW070154080526
44586CB00015B/1984